Module 1 • Set 1 • Get Ready: Fall

CONTENTS

This book belongs to

. . . .

GREAT MINDS

Great Minds® is the creator of *Eureka Math*™, *Wit & Wisdom*®, *Alexandria Plan*™, and *PhD Science*™.

Geodes™ are published by Great Minds in association with Wilson Language Training, publisher of Fundations®.

Credits

- *Seed Stash*: More page, Ron Rowan Photography/Shutterstock.com

- *Cranberry Crop*: front and back covers, Jena Ardell/Moment Open/Getty Images; title page and p. 3, Heidi Besen/Shutterstock.com; pp. 0–1, B Brown/Shutterstock.com; p. 2, A.J. Watt /E+/Getty Images; pp. 4–5, Christopher Boswell/Shutterstock.com; pp. 6–7, YinYang /E+/ Getty Images; pp. 8–9, BanksPhotos /E+/Getty Images; p. 10, Pgiam /E+/Getty Images; p. 11, Noppawat Tom Charoensinphon/Moment/Getty Images; p. 12, Orest_U/Shutterstock.com; p. 13, Michael Sean O'Leary/Shutterstock.com; More page, Danita Delimont/Alamy Stock Photo

- *Leaves*: We extend our thanks to the young artist, Alexander Maddox, who contributed his illustrations to this book; More page, Jakinnboaz/Shutterstock.com

- *Born to Fly*: More page, BlueRingMedia/Shutterstock.com

SEED STASH

written by
LAUNIE GARDNER

illustrated by
JEN CORACE

The sun is out. I am quick.

I dash up a tree trunk.

I jump from branch to branch.

Zig, zag, whiz! I cut pine cones.

Plop, plop, plop! They drop.

The stack is very tall.

The cones are full of seeds. I lug them to my stash.

Some drop on the way.

I dig a pit to hide them.

The seeds must last until spring.

There is not one bug or berry

to munch in winter.

A frost has come!
I grab grass and sticks
for another nest.

4

I have one nest by a stump and one in a log.

I make a new nest in a hole in a tree.

Two hawks skim the tree top above me. They want me in their claws for a snack.

"*Scat, SCAT!*"
I yell from a branch
and almost fall.

I rush into my log
to hide.

7

OCTOBER 30

Twigs snap—
my sis is here!

She wants to snatch my seeds.
I stamp my feet and flick my tail.

8

"*Chuck, chuck, chuck,*"

I grunt.

My bluff works!

She runs to her nest.

NOVEMBER 3

There is less light each day.

Each gust of wind is chilly.

I rest more and eat less.

I do not want my harvest to shrink in a blink.

11

NOVEMBER 17

I look out from my nest
to see snow fall.
I scan the land for pests.
All clear!

I dig up a cone.

I crunch and seeds fall out.

Chomp, chomp, yum!

I flop into my nest.

I nap on and off until long days come back.

MORE

Red squirrels prepare for winter by gathering and storing food during the fall. They often stash their food in many places rather than saving it all in one spot. Red squirrels use their keen sense of smell to find their hidden snacks. They can even locate buried seeds under 12 feet of snow.

If their supply of seeds and nuts runs low, squirrels will seek other sources of food. Red squirrels use their teeth to scratch the bark of maple trees. Their teeth poke holes through the bark, so the fluid can drain out. This sap sits in the sun and gets thicker. Squirrels return to lick this sugary syrup. It gives them much-needed energy during the winter months.

Cranberry Crop

by Mamie Goodson

It is a crisp fall day. Leaves crunch on our path down to the bog. There, red cranberries hang thick on vines.

I am a cranberry grower. It is harvest season on our farm. This is when we bring in our crop.

We do not pick the red berries by hand. We use water to help us. We call it a wet harvest.

First, we fill the bog with water. We bring the water up over the vines.

Next, we dip down into the bog on big harvest machines called water reels. They spin and swish through the water.

Cranberries drop from the vines. *Plip, plop.* They bob to the top of the water.

Our next job is to collect the berries. We splash into the bog. Red berries bob up and down, up and down. We drag them into one big batch.

Then, we pump the cranberries from the bog. We send them up a ramp into the truck. Jets of water flush out sticks and stems.

The berries bump along. They spill
into the truck bed, a rich red splash.
Plink, plink, plunk. Full to the brim
with berries, the truck can now set off.

The next stop is a big plant.

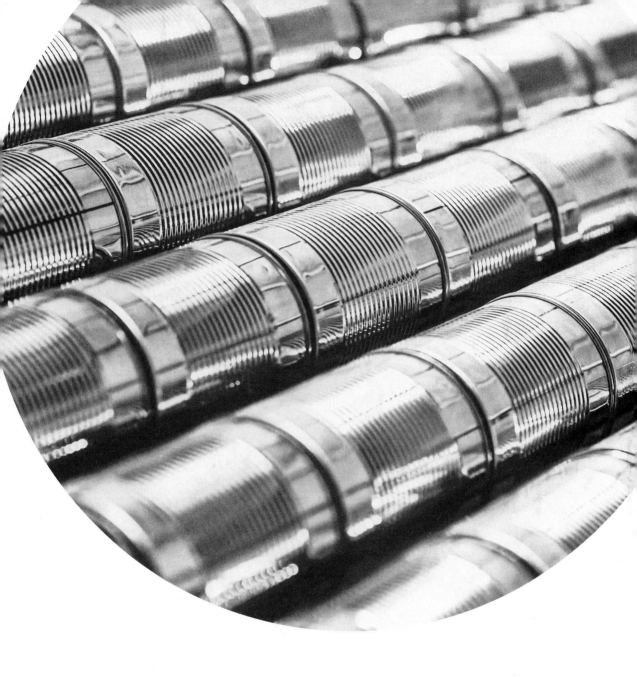

There, they will be made into
jam, juice, and sauce.

When the harvest is over, we will fill
each bog again with water.

This will help the small red buds
survive the winter frost. They will
become next year's cranberry crop!

Make Your Own Cranberry Relish

Ingredients

- 1 bag of fresh or frozen cranberries
- 1 tart green apple
- 1 stalk of celery
- 1 orange
- ¼ cup honey
- 1 to 2 teaspoons orange juice (optional)

Steps

1. Ask an adult to help you make the relish. Start by washing the cranberries and drying them with a paper towel.

2. Grate the zest from the orange into a small bowl. Cut off remaining pith (white part) from the orange. Then, cut the orange into small pieces.

3. Wash and core the apple. Cut into small chunks.

4. Wash the stalk of celery. Cut into small chunks.

5. Put the cranberries, apple chunks, celery chunks, orange zest, orange pieces, honey, and optional orange juice into a food processor or blender.* Blend until the mixture is finely chopped but not mushy.

6. Move the relish to a bowl. Refrigerate until serving time.

7. Enjoy!

If using a blender, consider making the relish in two small batches to avoid clogging the blade. Add 1 to 2 tablespoons of orange juice as needed.

More

Cranberries are native to North America. *Native* means "naturally living or growing in an area." The cranberries were not brought from somewhere else. Being a native plant, cranberries were a food source for American Indian tribes.

The Wampanoag and the Lenni-Lenape tribal nations on the East Coast and the Ojibwe near the Great Lakes have used cranberries for many purposes. The berries can be eaten fresh or dried. Cranberries are often a key ingredient in pemmican. Pemmican is a mix of dried meat, fat, and fruit that can be stored and eaten throughout the winter. In addition to being used as food, the fresh berries could be crushed and placed on wounds to help fight germs.

pemmican cakes

The Wampanoag still honor the importance of this native fruit. They celebrate Cranberry Day in October on Martha's Vineyard in Massachusetts.

LEAVES

BY RACHEL ZINDLER • ILLUSTRATIONS BY AMY HOOK-THERRIEN

The sun is out. It is a brisk fall day.

I pack my bag with a pad and a book

on trees. It is a good day to sketch.

1

I see each tree as it stretches over the path: the elm, the oak, and the maple. They stand tall and strong all year long.

Today they are a splash of fall colors! I stop to sketch each one. Many of their leaves rest on the grass. Little by little, they will all fall off.

I pick up one leaf from each of the
3 trees. They are all flat. They all
have lines called veins. Last spring,
they were all green. Now they are a
mix of colors. Each one has its own
shape, too.

4

The elm leaf is as gold as the fall sun. It is oval with a thin tip. Small veins stretch out from the midline.

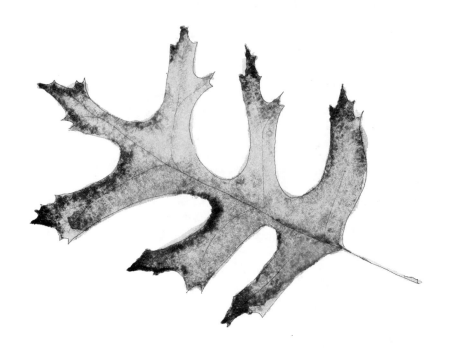

The oak is rust brown with a bit of red. It has 7 tips that stick out. The ends zig and zag. The veins come from the midline, too.

The maple is a hot red. It has
a hand shape. Many veins spring
out from the top of the stem.

The leaves have veins. But what do they do?

I scan my book. It says that veins help the tree stock up for the long winter. On a hot day, leaves catch sun and air and change them into food. The veins bring this food into the trunk. They also bring water up, to help the leaves grow.

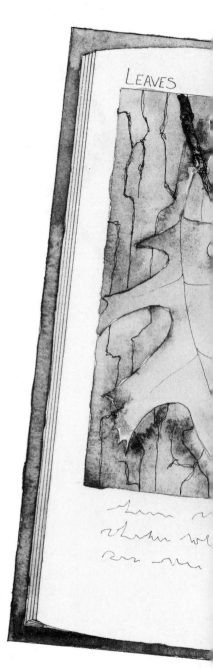

Soon, my trees will be bare. In the chill of winter, they will rest. When I come back, I will sketch just the bark on each trunk.

11

Then, in spring, the strong sun will be back. I will check out the buds. At last, fresh leaves will return.

13

In this spot there is something
new to sketch all year long.

14

MORE

Leaves produce most of the food a tree needs for the year during the sun-filled summer. The leaves use air, water, and sunlight to make food for the tree. This process is called photosynthesis. In the fall, there is less sunlight. Chemicals inside the tree sense this lack of light and start preparing for winter.

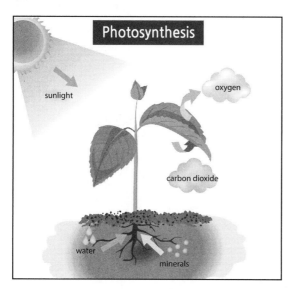

One important task of the preparation is to get rid of the leaves. This helps the tree save water and energy. It also protects the tree. Since the leaves are filled with water, they will freeze in the cold. Frozen leaves would hurt the tree. To push the leaves off, a tree grows special cells at the spot where the leaf is attached to the branch.

These cells cut the leaves off from the rest of the tree and block the water that flows up from the roots. The leaves dry up and fall off. A tree that loses its leaves for part of the year is called a deciduous tree. In the spring, the tree will grow new leaves.

Born to Fly

written by **Emily Goodson**

illustrated by **Juan M. Moreno**

The sun is out on a fall day. In the north, the frost will hit. The monarch butterfly must begin her long trip.

Each wing is strong. She
was born to fly.

She will set off from the branch of a tree.
Down, down, down—far from the slush
and crunch of the winter chill.

3

It is a long path. But she will not get lost.
Down, down, down.

Many monarch butterflies go to Mexico to spend the winter. Others fly to California.

To rest, she can ride a gust of wind.
She will drift over rich land... over
brick and brush, over bank and bend.
She can fly 100 miles each day.

She will make her way down
to the forests of Mexico.
There the day is still long.
She will find her mate.

6

In the spring, she will go north. Up, up, up! She will not survive the full trip back. She must stop and lay her eggs. Then she will die.

9

A new butterfly will pick up her
path. Up, up, up! She too will drift
with the sun . . . over brick and
brush, over bank and bend.

11

Like the last butterfly, she will stop and lay her eggs.

And just like the last, she will die. A new butterfly will take up the path.

Back and forth, spring and fall. Each monarch will do her part. It is a long trip. But they were born to fly!

More

The life cycle of a monarch butterfly has four stages: egg, larva, pupa, and adult.

To begin the cycle, a female monarch lays between 300 and 500 eggs on milkweed plants over several weeks. She usually lays only one egg per plant. It takes about four days for an egg to hatch.

Once the egg hatches, a butterfly larva, or caterpillar, appears. A caterpillar's main goal is to eat. It grows the most during this stage.

Next, the caterpillar enters the pupa stage by forming a chrysalis. The monarch develops within this sleeping bag-like sack. Eight to fifteen days later, a butterfly emerges from the chrysalis. Now the monarch has become an adult.

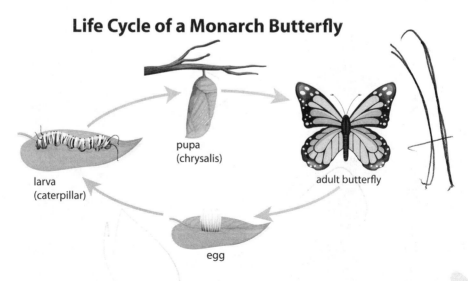

Life Cycle of a Monarch Butterfly

pupa
(chrysalis)

larva
(caterpillar)

adult butterfly

egg

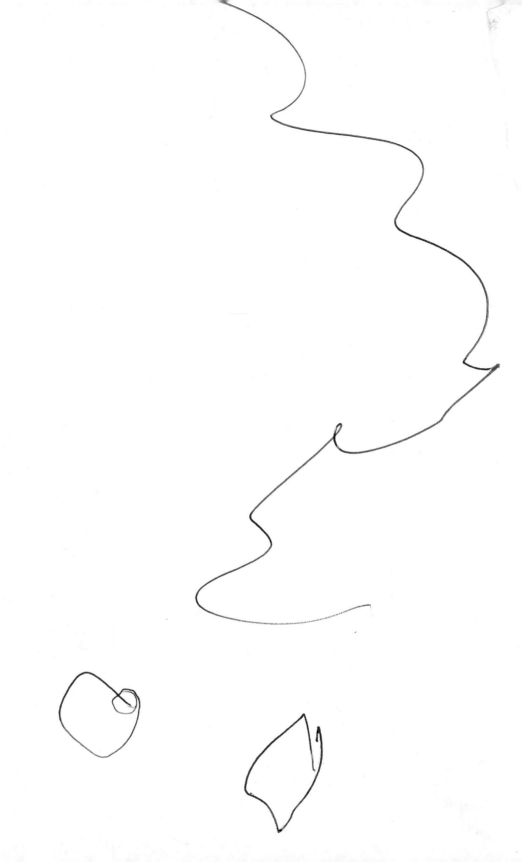